Monday After the End of the World

Monday After the End of the World

Poems by

Jim Zola

Cover design by Shay Culligan

ISBN: 978-1-952326-39-4

Kelsay Books
502 South 1040 East, A-119
American Fork, Utah, 84003

for Dylan, Ariana and Ethan

Acknowledgments

Many thanks to the following publications where some of these poems first appeared.

Aberration Labyrinth, Better Than Starbucks!, Loch Raven Review, Main Street Rag, Front Porch Review, Cincinnati Poetry Review, Florida Review, Mocking Heart Review, Blue Bonnet Review, Sweet Tree Review, Anomaly Literary Journal, Glint Literary Journal, Poetry Pacific, Corvus Review, 99 Pine Street, The Lake, The Drunken Llama, Full of Crow, Peacock Journal, Ghost City Press, The Bangalore Review, The Big Windows Review, Vending Machine, These Fragile Lilacs Poetry Journal, The Knicknackery, Poems-For-All, Dunes Review, Moledro Magazine, The Book Ends Review, Whimper Bang Journal, Futures Trading, Wink—Writers in the Know, Cabildo Quarterly, EHU—Edge Hill University Press, The Virginia Normal, Oyster River Pages, Varnish: A Journal of Arts and Letters, S/Word, Serving House Journal, Sleet.

Several of these poems first appeared in the chapbook, *The Hundred Bones of Weather* (Blue Pitcher Press).

Contents

Hours We Keep

A Mad Perhaps

In the Schenectady of the Mind

If it's metaphor
you want, I'm plumb out.
I'm through pounding sadness
into little blue bottles.
Similes slink
beneath dirty knives,
rust flavored forks.
I've stored my clichés
in the safe behind
the print of dogs
playing poker.

My alacks high-tailed it
in the middle of the night.
When the car dies,
I'll ride an old red bike
Owsley wild through the streets
of this done town,
pants cuffs rolled.
When they steal the bike,
I'll hoof it
till the tongues
of my shoes go dumb.

Hours We Keep

I have discovered that most of the beauties of travel are due to the strange hours we keep to see them.
From *January Morning* by William Carlos Williams

The Beauty of Falling

I watch from my kitchen window
as I wash evening dishes,
drink my first cup of coffee
each morning. The children spend
hours in that upstairs room. Bored,
they throw things out the window.
Paper floats gracefully
or flutters like a wounded bird.
Books flap, thud. Clothing falls
with the most flair—a pair of jeans
catches the wind with high kicks,
a t-shirt with words on the front
glides into the cool spring grass.
There seems to be a purpose
to what they drop.
They are learning things,
the beauty of falling.
Then I'm in the children's room.
The girl knows I'm something different.
Yellow and soft, a cotton blouse.
She picks me up, leans out
the window and tosses me
into the darkness. I fall
all night, a star turning
in the black sky. The girl sits
on the windowsill. I'm afraid
she'll fall hard, but she jumps
away and flies towards me.
Then we are falling together.

The Housewife Dreams the Drifter

Here beneath the hems
of evergreen, beside
the weathered shed
where sunlight doesn't reach,
the housewife squints
and takes it all in
until she sees him
standing near the broken
bones of railroad track,
smoking, staring back.

Last week she searched
each morning after
dropping off the kids.
When he didn't appear
in her rearview mirror,
or rise from the cold
exhaust of some
delivery truck,
she began to leave
her bedroom window
open through the night,
to leave the door
unlatched, to make
winding tracks through
the woods, dropping gifts
of homemade bread,
spit-shined apples, a split
of wine uncorked
on the back porch.

One day she undresses
and leaves her clothes
in a pile beside

the snow, dances
naked beneath the pine
boughs, gathers brush and twigs
to build a hut around
a bed of rags and straw,
burns dried lavender
and roses in a tin
bucket by the door.
The tracks she finds
are just her husband's
taking out the trash.
In dreams he comes.
She fixes the broken
split-rail fence, sets a trap
to keep him in.

A Poem that Starts in the Middle and Ends of Course

In the middle I pack a dark suitcase
—a handful of tiger's-eye marbles, a map
of your inner thigh, mornings where I wake
to the weeping of widows, books filled
with lyrical warrants, the blemished fabric
of youth. There are reasons for remembering.
Somewhere sits a life and key ring, but no clue
as to which metal desk, which rusted padlock,
which old shed they might open. Desire
to discover ends in a doorless room.
The nurse plans her escape, hoping to catch
Desperate Housewives. Finally
a commercial for Jell-O makes me think
of the lingering sadness that roosts in the corners
of hot rooms. We insist on interfering
with the order of things. When I say things,
I mean life. When I say life, I mean
the end of it, of course.

Box of Stars

Truth is that box of stars my kids press
on the bedroom ceiling. Shine a light
and they glow a little in the dark.
Then they stop no matter how much light
you give them. They fall one by one.
My father told a story about how he cut off
a man's ear and stuffed it in his pocket.
When I was seven, the doctors
wanted to break both my legs to fix them.
They bowed just like my father's did.
Standing side by side we made an M.
Mother told the doctors *No*. She wore
her anger like a scarf. Father
talked with both hands, grabbing air.
I thought if I could see the shapes,
I might understand his logarithms
of happiness. At eighteen, I ate
a paper star, saw colors in a lover's face
that weren't there before or after.
I walked my dog along the broken notes
of railroad tracks, memorized each missing
spike, her favorite spots for squatting.
I walked in shoes of blood. I walked away
from love so many times I ended up walking
back to it. When my father died,
I searched his pockets and found the stars.

Vicarious

The x-ray technician gently
touches my sides, moves me inches
so I am right for the view.
It's almost loving. She handles
patients all the time. *So you were in
a car wreck, pneumonia, troubles
climbing the stairs. Big breath and hold it.
Now you can breathe.* I exhale,
long to be touched again.

In My Sickness

I float above myself,
a gambler who has lost
everything twice. Below
shop windows fill
with dusty instruments.

When I push open
the door, a bell rings
off-key. The old lady
behind the counter
is a balloon
in dark fabric.

Somewhere,
a cat sleeps.

My dog isn't tired
but flops on the floor
wherever I stop.
She growls and stares.

She knows there are things
we cannot see.

The Bass River Fish Market

There was a marble-mouth cadence
to the names along the two-lane
highway down the Cape's gradual fold—
Braintree, Mashpee, Sandwich, Barnstable.
The last summer without worry,
I slept on beaches during the day,
slipping into the nightly chaos
of the Bass River Fish Market.
The stink of shrimp and grease weighed down
my clothes like an anchor. Butterflying
100 pounds of jumbos, heads lopped
with a blade sharp enough to subtract
a digit, picking the black ribbon
intestines wiped on an apron
stained with fish guts and blood like a flag
for a nation dedicated
to the lonely notions of pot washers
and prep cooks. This was a life for some.
What I remember about that summer
I could have made up. As I swing
my two children in the backyard,
I realize none of this will last.
Even now, as the light lingers
through broken trees, I want to hold it.
I push the swing back and forth.
They beg to go higher, faster.
All I want to do is slow it down.

A Poem Written in the Late Style of Myself

Blackbirds flap backwards
into morning mud.
Crow you say.
I am not sitting at a desk
sharpening the lead pencil of my father's death
or looking out a window
at childhood blooming incessantly
or even driving
blind in love with sight.
Write you say
the last thing written.
I'm stuck in thought—
three cold strawberries on a blue plate.
Eat you say.
Stain your fingers
before the birds return.

Coming to Terms

At night, once-dark windows flicker yellow light,
forcing me to imagine lives sadder than my own.

She wears pink fuzzy slippers. A dog bowl lost
in the corner. She believes in radio

romance. Her husband is dust gingerly moved
between crystal angels. She wonders why

I conjure her instead of a hootchie mama
in a snug slip eating buttered crackers,

dancing to the rhythm of her own sweet sway.
She imagines me across the mud shaven field,

the rabbit loved emptiness, this doom that connects us.

Becoming Trout

I spend years of my life in dusty warehouses
dreaming about women who will never love me.
I whisper lies in the sweaty afterglow
of sex. I practice love by call and response.
When my father's heart stops without notice,
I feel a fishbone stuck in my throat and know
my last chance to speak has passed.
My gills pulse. Water rises.

Supplication

I count food trucks lined by the curb
on my drive home. Hunger fogs
my windows as I long
for sweet chicory brew
or syrupy vodka sloshed
in a jelly jar.

Arriving to an empty house
is a luxury I cannot
afford. I try to explain
to my kids how this endless dance,
this living from can't see
in the morning to can't see

at night is reason enough.
I'm not a good liar.
Tonight, when I pull in
the driveway, I sit and listen
to some concerto
in B flat minor.

If I open the door,
the music will die.
Through the passenger window
I watch a squirrel chittering
warnings. Looking up I see
a red-shouldered hawk looking back.

Blade

When my father died my mother traveled
untethered as if he were the rope
and death the cutting blade.

One summer I pulled a buck knife on a boy
who bullied me. The black handle
a perfect fit for my fist, I flipped

the blade to let him see and hoped
my shaking was taken as passion,
as I do now, still. When the first girl I loved

dumped me, I walked through a plate glass door
and saw the white bone of my ankle
like a whispered secret. Years later,

she emails from Guatemala to say
she is part of the revolution,
that I revolt her and should stay far away.

My mother phones from Alaska to ask
if I need a new winter coat.
When my father's heart stopped, while he shopped

at the mall, the paramedics sliced
his down ski jacket from top to bottom.
I know because I saw it hanging

like a tired flag of surrender
in my mother's closet that first Christmas
she spun out into the world without him.

God Is in the Details

Waiting at the dentist for my name
to be called, I thumbed through issues
of Highlight Magazine, entranced
by the hidden picture puzzles.
A toaster in the trees, a chickadee
in a pig's ear, a wrist watch ticking
in jungle moss. These days, I find
what brings me joy is the details noticed.
I search for the fork hidden
in gravel, the needle in the man's
clenched fist, a face in the too blue sky.

In the Boarding School of Air

My kids have a toy where they sit
and spin, then stand up and stagger,
laughing, drunk on air. I want that.
I want to change my name
to *abracadabra,* change my address
to *are we there yet.* On my drive

to work I pass heavy equipment
that scrapes the earth, pass workers dressed
in orange suits as they loiter
between breaks. Some smile, some glare.
They know more than I.

Bagworms dress the branches
of evergreens. My mouth is full
of dead things. I hop on one foot.
Then I'm spinning around
in nothingness, waiting
for the world to start.

Milosz's Bees

Bats in the belfry, bats in the belfry.
 Who is the dictator of madness?
  Who deems the muddled coherent enough?
I smile when I ask. I had a wife and children once.

Bees fill a hole in my backyard, their sudden home.
 One day it's safe, the next they swarm, sting the dog.
  At dusk I sneak with gasoline, boiling water.
Smoke them out. These are not gentle bumblebees.

Night by night I fill the hole. Nothing around it is living.
 But they survive. I stay inside. I listen.
  The children are back. I press my ear against glass.
What are they singing? A song for the end of the world.

My Daughter's Day in Court

For now the sky agrees
with me. One enormous
stratus, a hint of rain.
I'm going over my list
of worries. Check, check, check.
None amiss. This morning
I told my daughter to dress
appropriate for the occasion.
She wears a maroon skirt,
work boots and a Beatles top.
All she wants is to stay
in bed twenty-four seven.
Even when she is gone,
the shape of her stays behind.
Later, I promise
I will take her to the movie
she is dying to see,
where we will sit in the hushed
dark, forgot our worries
and come out to a night
that is at least forgiving.

After Reading an Ad for a Breathing Machine

The dog follows, room to room. When I rise,
she is ready to move as though tethered

by invisible thread. My son is learning
to lie. It's expected. He just turned five

at a party where he was king. He says
he didn't do it. Today the sun is gray

and avoids the sky. I saw an ad
for a breathing machine in mint condition,

only used a few days. I said goodbye
to my father twice. The first time,

at a restaurant in Rhinebeck, my mother leaned
into me and whispered he doesn't have long

to live. In the quiet of this house, I count
each breath. The dog's legs pedal in sleep as if

she is inches from the squirrel she'll never catch.
I lied. I never said goodbye.

Separation

If you summon it by the right word, by its right name, it will come.
—Kafka

Today is the first day
of sun in a week. I'm blinded
as I walk out my front door,
stumble on the steps that lead
to my other life.

There I'm a sailor with gold
in my ear. There I'm made
of paper and fly.
There we linger
until the alphabet
of our passions defines us.

When Columbus sailed
over the edge, birds searched for names.
Corvus brachyrhynchos flops.
Cyanocitta cristata screams
jee ah jee ah. Columbus fell.

Weeding my flower bed,
I think of Empress Dowager
Cixi on her walks to the garden.
Servants dove under the pond to hook
her fishing line with koi.
If her scowl was deep enough,
jewelry was the catch.

I'm not a fisherman.
My son thinks to fish means to slump
on a muddy bank eating slices
of baloney.

But once
when we found a farmer's pond
beyond the swiss-cheese no
trespassing signs, each time
he dropped his line, a tiny
painted turtle tugged. Halfway up,
the turtle let go. Again and
again they played this scene
until our laughter spread out
past noxious weeds into fields
to stun the lull of just
waking cows.

My daughter is a hugger.
I take out the trash and when
I come back she greets me
like I've been gone for days.

Why do we eschew sentiment?
I love my daughter's signs of love.

The racket rises from trees
behind my house.
I pity

the hidden owl. Crows mock
from low branches and later
snack on beetle grubs in lawn
sod, or pull the liver
from road-kill squirrel.
I'm told they mate for life.

My wife and children fly
into the sky without me.

We Give Back What We Cannot Keep

Better to begin at noon with bricks instead of river rocks,
with three train crossings we call the bones of Mister Jones,
with a river that rises in locks, with a father who works
at the ice factory and brings home sculptures, nudes reduced
to acceptability, swans without wings,
with a mother whose hands are whiter than fishbone.
So we begin with departure and travel this distance
between us, as if to touch is to travel.
Or with sleep, sound, back to back. When I wake,
I am three and flying around the basement,
my shoes scuff the red cement floor, my legs
are braced. Father kneads them with his icehouse hands.
We give back our mothers and fathers, sweat fresh
on their faces, give back birds that rise from the thin
comfort of branch to shake the elms, give back the field's past.
Outside this window, there are no fields. There are warehouses,
the clatter of train and track, and warehouse birds.
They hop on corrugated rooftops.
They sing for our leaving.

Trying to Write a Poem about My Mother

There's a beginning and an end and a yard
with toys scattered like little car wrecks,
a dirty truck, stegosaurus with its head

gnawed off. In the corner I notice
an elderly woman. She is older than she looks
and she inspects the few straggly chokeberries

that grow there as if reading footnotes.
She asks why I only write about him.
Because you're still alive. She laughs and holds out

her hands, empty and green. The elms are full
of crows. That's how I know
it's time for me to get to work.

Trying to Come to Terms with My Daughter's Depression

I have been here before
and don't remember this exact
line of trees, the way branches

on the ground, leaves, seem out of place.
The dog barks at nothing, her hackles
mohawk in attempt to appear

a threat. What ghosts are these?
I am thinking about
Koudelka's gypsies, how they

all have dirty hands, faces,
a sadness they seem proud
to possess. What can I say?

Sometimes you get tired of the dark.
There are songs too wide for sound.
No one easily survives love.

Empirical

Sometimes a word is like the sound
a wind chime makes in the neighbor's yard
where all you ever hear is barking,
a dog you never see but imagine—
a mutt with one black eye, one brown
and a dusty snout snuffing
at the bottom edge of the privacy fence
that keeps him in. What evidence
is needed? One plus one plus one.
Look through the wooden slat, whisper
loving sounds. Somewhere there is an empire
and a miracle and a hound
head back, baying at the truth.

I Have Walked Long in this Night without Absence

I believe the shadow
of a bird crossing my window

is enough
warbler jackdaw shrike
darkening
the floor of this room

survivors
nesting in cigarette packs

box seats on power lines
in my next to last life I want to return

as a common coot
running on top of cool water
I have walked long in this
night
that always ends
with the hymn of our flesh

Elegy with Four Walls and a Crack in the Ceiling

Five days into the theory of decay,
the Plecostomus disintegrates
at the touch of a swooping net, becomes
the rot it was assigned to control.

In the lobby of the Tiger Hotel,
dust finds permanence in high eaves
the desk clerk with a birthmark on his neck
might have noticed once, as he watched daylight
paint each slow square of stucco. The clerk
doodles on scraps. Ten years from now he'll be dead
from a disease that, on this day, has no name.

In this house with a tank diminishing
in population, your son notices
a crack in the ceiling. You might tell him
a story, this story. When he asks
what will happen if the house collapses,
what should you answer? When is truth not enough?

A Mad Perhaps

The heart of man is hardened by infatuation,
a faulty advisor, the first link to sorrow...
                                    —Aeschylus

Last Call

In Burnt Hills, New York,
where I was born,
the mad lived out of town,
just far enough. Smoke
from their chimneys darkened
the snow that fell
on our shoulders
as we huddled
at the playground
and warmed our hands
inside our jacket sleeves,
and swore at the dead
who were warmer than us.
We were children until
someone told us we weren't.
The mad never grew old,
they never raced their cars
on Blue Barn Road,
or drank themselves dizzy
summer nights behind
the high school. But the mad
travelled closer until
the distance between their words
was all we noticed.
I remember three horses
and a distant field,
how a girl we both loved
talked with the shy one,
as if to a child
bruised by the hands
of too much darkness.
She talked about its beauty,
the way weather became
part of the mane.

It believed the voice
and nuzzled her hands
empty of sugar,
licking the skin's salt
as if each finger
might hold the secret
to another mine
deep within the body.
If the girl went mad
that day in the field
of horses, I did not
notice. Her sadness
seemed ordinary.
Now, years later,
you tell me she did.

Slipping

The house is slipping down the slope.
He can tell—less lawn to mow.
It nudges a shiver, an eyelash,
a whisper, a grass blade tip.
At first, he says nothing.
When he finally
speaks up,

his family blames age. They smile, say
they'll take a look. He looked years ago.
The dahlia, planted by his wife
one spring when her crouched shape still sprung
green lust within him, persevered
until cinderblock was too much.
Sometimes, he dreams he's on a ship—
the foundation shakes loose anchors
and he floats away from dirty snow.
Other times, he gets angry, resists
the slow moving force. He stands
with his back against the wall
to push. Neighbors think he's resting.
How would they know he's trying
to stop a house?

Harmony and the Birds

Chickadees fluff
outside the surgeon's office
against a backdrop of dark
pine and sky where I
imagine an owl sleeps
in a hollow dream of feathers.
The middle of this poem
is missing, the part
where the poet reveals
something. Perhaps he longs
to kiss the silver chain
around the gypsy's ankle,
or marks x's
on the calendar
stopping at the date
of his own death,
or slowly slices
an over-ripe tomato
and remembers
his mother's hands.
The birds of course
always come back to the poem.
It's like one of those puzzles
we did as children,
waiting in the doctor's office,
find what's missing,
the hidden pictures
in pages of a magazine.
Later, much later,
a cardinal lands
on the iron back
of a patio chair
outside my bedroom window.
Its beak opens

and closes, opens
and closes. A song
I can't hear. Yet I find myself
opening and closing my mouth
in harmony.

Falling for the Invisible Woman

The obvious is what's missing,

cues like shaved legs, make-up, the secret
smile. Her voice turns heads, it chimes
like rosaries across her lips.
No that's not it. But sometimes at night
I think I hear her while I sleep.
Her friends, all men with special powers,
shun the one who can't do anything
beyond a few card tricks,
a double-jointed thumb.
Even their alter-egos—
rich playboys, business tycoons,
brilliant scientists—shadow me.
When I ask her to slow dance,
Plastic Man stretches an arm between us,
The Human Torch fires nasty looks.
In bed between tangled sheets,
she strokes my scars and wants a story.
How many lies are new lovers allowed?
Come morning,
I whisper her name in every room.

A Poem in Which My Father Refuses to Appear

Service trucks rattle by
ladder topped with tools
on a mission to fix whatever is broken.
I catalog roadside trash,
empty bottles empty wrappers,
each a clue.
I'm wintering
or maybe I just like the term.
Counting the days—one, two, many.
When I get there
I'll know.

My daughter thinks
dinosaurs passed pilgrims
    the hallway
      xtinction.
    ə , inks I wax
  ⅃e floors
with a rag of my life.
As kids, we tried to get lost
riding bikes into neighborhoods
beyond the boundaries
our mothers set. There was no
particular darkness then.
Just dogs yapping at our heels
as we pedaled like hell
towards the next block.
The body
belongs to no one. My life is orbed by death's
dark moons. Ring tones turn ominous.
When I die, play gypsy music,
violin and cimbalom.

This morning
while merging onto Wendover Ave,
I watched a Cooper's hawk
thunk to earth ungraceful
in the overgrown median
in pursuit of something I couldn't see.
Later crows took over.
One is sorrow.
One foot stuck in a dead squirrel's guts.

The Girl behind the Tree

As I drive my kids to school,
a girl stands behind a tree
halfway up Centennial.
She's leaning or hiding.
One time I saw her face
as she peeked around the edge.
It was covered with long black hair.
She's waiting for the bus
by herself. She has her reasons
for standing behind
that particular tree

each morning, just as I have
my reasons for flying out
of the house holding a cup
of warm coffee, yelling
at the kids. I find myself
making up stories for her -
the cryptic notes she hides
in her pockets, dark corners
of her room, the way she hates
her mother's smile. I'm sorry.
I know some morning I'll drive past
the tree and she'll be gone.
That's when I'll wave.

The Man in the White Jeep

I lean and like the way bark feels
against my skin, my bones, through my clothing.
The other kids stopped coming to this corner.
I look at my hands and see movies, my hair
like a curtain. Sometimes I hear birds

in the trees, but never see them.
Then the man in the white jeep drives past.
I stare at my feet. I know he'll return.
The birds tell me. If I lean hard enough
against the tree, I might disappear.

Living Next-door to the Firebug

He hides behind brick, the clever pig.
My castle is clapboard, a tinderbox
with dusty windows. When I strike
a match to light the patio grill,
his curtains rustle. All kids are pyros,
the leaf pile smudging adolescence,
newspapers curled into a wisp of print
as though the stories sprout wings.
But most of us lose the flame
when other things stoke our passions.
Not him. I catch my neighbor gathering
twigs in oily sacks. Smoke that rises
from chimneys all down the block
is whitish gray and hugs the limbs
of trees. His chimney bellows black,
angry at the sky. Some mornings I find
spent matches lined like soldiers along my walk.

The Firebug Finds Love

If they made a sulfur scented aftershave, I'd rock it.
But I seldom need to shave. The man next door hides
behind a beard. He sneaks outside to smoke cigarettes,
an occasional cigar, puffed to the nub
and gathered in a plastic solo cup. He sniffs
the air as if he might sense me behind the window's shade.

My earliest memory was playing in the fire pit
on camping trips; trapping beetles between the red hot logs
until they sizzled, popped. I've never had a real girlfriend,
but the checkout girl where I get my matches
is as beautiful as a butterfly in flames.

The Singing Bone

—after the Italian folktale

I am somebody's son, buried
in a field, waiting for your
wrinkled hands to dig me out
of earth that refuses nothing,
to shake off the dirt's dullness
and hold me against your lips,
to sing my body's song
through the heavy reeds
of your body, from one side
of the heart to the other
and back again. I would tell you
all I remember, the names
of the guilty, the different names
for guilt. But you wouldn't
listen, the words would turn to stones
beneath cool water, or blossom
into a language even
the fish refuse. So I'll sleep
in this field until dirt
replaces the words of my song,
until memory becomes
tangled with the roots of plants
that have no needs. Maybe
I'll never wake to realize
I'm whole again, that these bones
lean against the cool flesh
of darkness. Passing above,
will you recognize what's buried?
If you stop to listen, will you
understand this song, the years
it took to compose, how it's
only your harmony that can still me?

What the Feral Boy Might Tell

They caught me scrounging tubers
 in a field. I was expected
to have the sense to die, left
pig-stuck in a thicket,
my father's signature—
a jagged scar across my neck.

Farmers' wives claimed they saw me
howling at an empty sky.
Lies. Curled in a fetal wrap,
I dream of Psamtik,
the lonely room. I fool them all.

They poke me with their simple hopes,
torture me for speech. Eau, the glass
half-filled but out of reach.
Idiot. I shine the apple
of debate, piss wherever I please.
I fill a cart with dung and then,
unstopped, shovel it unfilled again.

To show me off, I dine
with generals and dark eyed
intellects. I wolf each course,
stuff my fancy pockets
with desserts, then slip away,
strip my outer skins to leap
through gardens, agile as
a maddened squirrel.

Book of Giants

In dreams I see trees as men walking.
I wake, punch the sky. Dumbness
is a blessing. In one palm I hold
feathers and have no idea where I
got them. The boy in the lake looks up
at me, muddy eyes through sedge.
I want to touch him but know he has fallen
for good reason. Instead, I gobble
my breakfast, ten moonpies, wrappers and all.

The Giant Holds a Persimmon

Snakes peek out of holes. I lick lips,
listen for thunder, skull smacked.
Anger comes from a pain more specific than
detractors could ever imagine. Bad teeth,
a back unforgiving. Mumbling apologies
to furry things crushed beneath my toes,
I bend to pick the one ripe fruit. So tiny, it hides
in the folds of my palm. Suddenly my heart
begins to ache. I know I need to be going.

The Boy in the Lake

That moonpie face stares down
at me, his fallen angel.
How wrong can one be? I open
my mouth to call for help, minnows
eclipse my cry. He opens his mouth
drowning in sky. My breakfast
again is downy and quacks.
Distorted by a watery sun,
his smile floats gigantic.

The Giant Laments

I poke darning needles through the loose skin
of my elbows, stiff leg it down roads pocked
with horse dung piles bigger than a breadbox.
How small the hills appear when I squint
and squat in ditches. Children skipping past
make my stomach pit. Their laughter stones me.
I want to return to the womb of the well,
to linger in gypsum, finger the fragments. This
is the way the world ends—the giant winks.

The Silence

When a tree falls, a snowy owl rents the silence;
the moon reflecting white on the blade
of a knife that slices off a banker's thumb
in Buenos Aires. His scream falls on ears
that prefer to hear other things. Starlings carry
silence through tangled catalpa branch.
The thumb finds a bed in a velvet cigar box
in the Cleveland den of a middle-age salesman,
scoping gloomily online for such odd finds.
He brags and shows off to Miss Sarah Deakins,
a second grade teacher who swears her heart almost stops
as he unveils the shriveled digit and reads
from a mimeographed sheet that arrived,
UPS, with the thumb. Later, all she can
think of as she slips into bed, is the way
the box still carried the odor of tobacco.
She remembers summers at Gramma K's in Kernersville,
where she first tasted the hot stream from a cow's teat,
first felt the spin from a cigarette laced with jimson weed,
first kissed the stink from a drunken boy's chest
as he pushed into her again and again,
muffling her cry with a hand that smelled like silence.

Monday after the End of the World

The Eskimo Curlew gave Columbus his sign
that land wasn't far, preventing mutiny,
staving off madness.
You look for signs, a modicum of oomph,
the song bugs in catalpa, magnolia,
bananas ripening on the kitchen counter,
almost black, still sweet,
light the lop-sided candle
in a dish on the dresser,
rub ointment into the scars
on her back and shoulders,
or play the untuned piano
notes that find
your fingers.
Jackdaw greets the sun rising
above the green mist, a stand
of pine, chattering in code—
fire, fire.
Someone
leaning in, whispers
in your sleeping ear—
gone, gone.

Friday after the End of the World

All there is left to eat is pumpernickel,
pumpernickel muffins, pumpernickel bread,
pumpernickel bagels. The sky can't make up
its mind. Leaves still waltz, some hint at a tango,
down to pavement that peeks up at the indecisive
sky. In between is akin to disaster
if disaster were a ginger with lacy sleeves
and a ring on every toe.

Monday Is Mulligan Stew

You say Monday after
the end of the world
is like a check engine light
coming on. We want
so much to ignore it.
I say do. I say
Monday is more
like mulligan stew.
I'll stoke the fire,
you pluck the hen.
Afterwards, we'll sing
about riding the rails,
then clean our nails
with splintered bones.

Birds of Appetite

You are requested to serve on the committee
of generalizations, to whisper sweet
ohs in the ear of some other horse,
to carve the metaphase of *I Am*
into your wife's blue ankle, to catalog
no-see-ums on the dead elk's snout.
We will not accept the usual excuses;
there is no body to be found, feather
is to summons as blood is to blister,
it was in my other jacket pocket,
my other skin left out. No no no no.
You are requested to serve biscuits
to the missing. Butter, jelly, jam.
They will eat eventually. You must wait.

Vespers for the Old World Sparrow

In the high court of sparrows
I plead my wants, turn on
every light switch, gather twigs
build a nest of sorrow

in the high nest of wants
I build sparrows, gather light,
court twigs of sorrow
plead every switch to turn

in the twigged light of nests
I court the plea of sparrows,
build high my wants, my sorrow,
turn, gather the switch

to strike the sparrow, to empty
the high nest, to gather fallen twigs,
to touch the still feather,
to plead my guilt in the court of sorrow

The Sadness of Wrens

Each year on the anniversary of his passing,
my father comes to me in a dream.
We talk like father and son,
ignoring the fact that he left life behind
like forgotten luggage
on a train station platform.
Last night in our conversation he told me
I had it wrong
But the numbers continue to add up.
Birthdays, bills, pins, pounds.
My wife laughs when I explain my theory of aging,
how it is the giving in that makes us old.
More laughter when I refer to the sadness
of wrens. Birdbrains, she says, no weeping.
But what about their song?
My mother gave me a crate full of old albums,
heavy black vinyl, dusty jazz, Russian masters,
light opera. In the confusion of sleeves,
I found a record labeled with my father's name—
Eugene. He recorded it sometime soon
after returning from the South Pacific,
in a sound booth where he sang
and paid for one copy. When I take it
to a friend who has the equipment to play
78's, we find it is too warped, scratched, faded.
I'm left wondering if it is full of the sorrow
I recall nesting in his voice those last years,
or joyful, glad to be alive.

Visible and Invisible

Lately I have been living here
between the invisible landscapes,
lost in the backyard gone lank with weeds.
But that's ok. What better way
to help my search for cures, for roots
and seeds - camel thorn, velvet bean,
wild cherry. Each uncovering
turns tonic, nervine for the soul.
Who's to say who will be the first
to go, lining up, the visible,
the invisible? Each day I find myself
stuck in-between, where only
the living wear shoes, where my mother
steams wild asparagus all morning
and my father sits and chews areca nuts,
where I know I will become visible
again after everything else has faded.

Crossing

Rattle blurs past; graffiti
two feet high in neon
green and orange, a cock
exploding.
I'm Biloxi bound,
I'm a bored teen tossing
my brother's shoes skyward.
I'm in your car snaking
my hand up your sundress
to rest on your inner thigh.
The Buick behind me
has someplace to go.
I take one last look
at the train disappearing
and think of the engineer
as he flicks an ash
and watches the same towns
pass. He thinks about lunch,
a nip at the flask
that makes the day fade
like a whistle. I'm the boy
kicking dirt by the side
of the tracks, train forgotten,
looking up at sneakers
that sway the line.

Riding in Back

Before safety mattered,
we rode in back
without seatbelts.
The radio never played
anything that rocked.
On long trips I became
an agent tracking secrets,
taking pictures with the camera
hidden inside my eyes.
I stared at the back
of my father's head,
his black hair starting to gray,
and fed him directions.
Always faster.
Sometimes it worked.
Usually we snailed along.
I can't remember when I discovered
I was a double agent,
when exactly I cracked the code,
the slight nod. Then I rode in front,
next to my father, with control
over the knobs. I become him,
a trick, wearing his clothing.
A voice in my head tells me
to drive faster. I resist.
Still the trees blur.

Dusk

You become home to your wife's sadness
in your inner ear, beneath your nails,
in skin sloughed off that turns to dust.
Cautious upon entering each room, as if
the empty hours still gathering might leap up.
Once you were younger and certain
of everything, which was nothing.
You wandered down by Hunter's Creek, crawling
in a cave, a rush of bats
surrounded you, kept coming.
Now the bats are in the attic
against eave slats in need of painting.
At dusk you hear their leaving.
You wish they would take this sadness too.

Other Ways the World Might End

My father hung a human ear from his belt.
Home from the war and many years later,
he refused to share the stories that roosted
on his shoulders like a roc. The blue
jacket in the closet is as close as we got,
gold buttons and mothball cologne. When he died,
I went deaf for a day. All lawnmowers stopped.
Back then the Mohawk stunk. Once, on a dare,
I stuck my toes in. They came out speckled,
tingling. We rode our Schwinns past the green lawn
of the Knolls Atomic Power Lab,
pedaling fast, afraid to breathe, lifting
our feet over the railroad tracks.
At Lock 7, when they flooded the channel

to raise a barge, we could scream our darkest
secrets and risk nothing. This is what
the end must sound like. My father took me there
to fish off cement walls, catching sunnies
as small as my hand. When I reeled-in
a hefty cat, my father sliced it open
to show the parts still working. I remember

how shiny it looked, the way he used the blade,
how I knew he wanted to tell me more.

Whatever Isn't Glory

The first thing I notice is how her hair smells like coffee.
She stoops to look shorter, holds cigarettes between thumb
and index fingers like a writer she admires.
She speaks with an accent perfected on the hogs.
For years she tried to distance herself from Missouri
farm life. But the heartland was a magnet
engineered to drag her back. Her husband spends hours
driving dirt roads or sitting in a hot car.
She looks through windows laced with curtains.
It never rains. I find myself making up stories
for her to tell. She married an explorer.
He gives islands and rivers her name. She waits
for the mail, for the letter saying he is lost.
And if they have children, they are seldom seen.
They hide behind the leaning barn. They whisper
flies off the bored swine's ears. She renames each child
for the things she discovers in her life.
They promise to return.

In the Schenectady of the Mind

I wasn't born as much as I fell out
—The Clash

In Your Absence

Yesterday was soup day, the kitchen a mess
of parts, turnips beheaded, tomatoes crushed.
Hot and sour, potato, stone soup, a cure-all
or just a distraction.
I suspect the kids are feeding the mouse on the sly,
left out slices of bread stale and nibbled. I too
hide behind an armory of mercy,
putting out the traps but forgetting to set them.
On my drive to work I watch the homeless parade
from a stand of trees to take their posts at each
street corner of the busy intersection.
I wonder about what isn't seen in that small patch
of wilderness. I think of a line from a poem I read
this morning—*he's made himself a study in the trees.*
Before the light turns green,
I'm one of Cabeza de Vaca's lost men
arriving to a gift of 600 open deer hearts,
emeralds. The explorer wrote about a poison
the natives gathered from a certain tree
so deadly that if animals drank from where bruised leaves
had been steeped, they would burst.
What I'm trying to say is I'm lost.
You are my Kashmir, not here,
not actually mine.
I've made myself a study in your absence.

On the Street Where I Grew Up

I'm in my old neighborhood
shortcutting though yards
never past the witches' house
once it rain frogs
& packing popcorn we thought
was snow
snow of course was snow
enough
snot on mittens
bombing the cars
on Grand Boulevard
hiding behind evergreens
thick with ice daggers
most of the houses
stayed dark inside except
for one room
old people lived there
couples or widows
and now I'm not sure
how much of what I remember
is made up
like the story of the bedridden man
cared for by his old wife
who served him his breakfast in bed
each morning until one morning
when he asked her what was
for breakfast
instead of pancakes
she took an axe from behind
her back
said *how about this*
and chopped him up
into little bits
maybe that was just

a story kids tell on the playground
when teasing
becomes boring
maybe the ambulance that parked
in front of the house
was there because the old man
had a stroke, heart
attack, seizure
or just gave up
living in one lit room
but I swear that night
when I looked out the window
the falling snow
was red

Lemons

How is it there are moments we hold
forever and others that go

quicker than the sulfur whiff
of a put out match. Who decides?

I want that job. To say
who will remember the mole

on a lover's shoulder
twenty-five years ago,

but forget her name, that you
will forget the way your mother's

voice sounded when she laughed,
but will remember the way

her hair smelled once during a fever
when she leaned over you

and said something you don't
remember, something about lemons.

Elsewhere

Lately I've been thinking about
Lock 7, the way we used it
as an escape, mesmerized
by the powers assumed, raising
and lowering the river,
of how we fished it
for bottom cat, mostly catching
sunfish the size of our hands,
throwbacks or keepers
in a bucket, slow deaths
we tried to reschedule,
hoping the hook wounds would heal
if we stared into the water
long enough. Most were lost
on the bike ride home
through winding shoulderless roads
with weeds whipping our faces,
through two tunnels, abandoned
railroad lines, arriving
with near-dry buckets
and sunfish drowning in air.

Jazz Hands

The most Italian thing about my father,
besides his black olive hair curly to the end,
and his ignitable temper, was the way
he talked with his hands, a kind of punctuation,
chops and dots as if painting the space
in front of him, as if his fingers were brushes.
An art. What I got from him, not the hair,
mine once thick and dish water blonde, now grey
going to white, is his language of gestures.
And his anger, not so much a gift,
but a giving. So I ended up teaching in a school
for the Deaf, learning to talk with my hands.
And I learned to channel my anger through
words on the page. At the dinner table, I try
out my jazz hands with my daughter. She laughs
and tells me I'm doing it wrong. *Those are spirit
hands.* And for the first time in years I feel
my father spark from the flesh of finger tips
and shoot around the blue kitchen walls.

My Mother Meets Ali

Thank you, Mr. Clay is what she said,
taking back the egg-stained napkin
with the boxer's scrawl brought home to me.
It was 1968
and the boxer might have struck a man
for calling him Clay. This middle-aged
suburban housewife showed no fear.

Fear is something boxers recognize,
pursue. My fears are simple, common,
the unnatural music of the heart.
When my firstborn learned to walk, going
from combat crawl to scoot, I struggled
to let him fall. So much effort. Tired,
he would lay with his ear to the ground
listening to the earth's inner-workings.

My mother's memory is a feather.
On the phone, she forgets my name.
She doesn't remember my first steps,
though she says she does. I have the napkin
tucked inside a book, the boxer's name faded.
My mother shows no fear. She calls me
by my father's name. I always answer.

Not Drowning

A boy at the bus stop
cups his hands to light
a cigarette in the rain.

You never want to wear
shoes again. But you
are a shoe. You want

to return as a bird,
the hummingbird
never seen. So the moon

wanes behind a fist
of clouds.
What you do not hear

builds until it deafens.
If you stare long enough
into the sway of trees,

you will see a body
of water. A fish jumps
into your arms. This song

of drowning.

from My Lost Journal

We engineered playground floods,
rescued ants on elm bark boats.
Now when I visit

even the witches' house
has lost its spell.

I smoke and think
possibly I am the smoke.
At dark's edge, monsters

couple with trees.
I brush your face
with the back of my hand

and see Eva Marie Saint,
the way she touched Brando.
Is it a sin

to believe when I close my eyes
the world darkens?

Philosophy on a Morning too Early for Disaster

Although the kitchen window is masked by grime,
cobwebs, morning light finds a way. It's this
persistence that keeps you going, the memories
like a black and white movie. Each year,
a few more frames are lost; most of the actors

gone. But in the day, they wore their hats jauntily
and drank from bar ware that never ran dry.
Maybe because despair was in the last drop.
You never finish a cup of coffee.
This morning is no different. Take your mug

to the sink, splash out the now cold liquid.
Gather your things. You think about leaving.
Stopped at the traffic light, you watch a crow
strut across the parking lot hauling half
a hamburger bun in its beak.

Trying to Write a Poem about Joan Blondell

Not knowing how or when, the poem becomes
a crystal ornament smashed beneath
a black boot heel, a son tossing
his father's bag-of-bones body
against the kitchen wall and later
regretting a broken plate. It's blue,
something his wife picked up at a yard sale
years before and in another town.
She said the plate once belonged
to a Russian Prince who ate canned peas
every day. The only time the Prince
was truly happy was when he picked
a bucket of ripe strawberries
in Horodok in June, the light
scattered through a net of dying branches.
The berries were delicious and red.
This is my assumption, my right
to assume. Your hair may have been
berry red for all I know. This
isn't a poem about that. It's about
light, the branch, the sound a plate makes
when it hits tile, the dry crack
of a thief's leg bone, the second nail
through the thin wrist, strawberries
served on a cracked blue platter
just before the movie begins.

My Reckling

Back then you refused the light,
wombstuck, and made the iron bed shake,
made the monitor mountain climb.
There is breath and there is breathing.
You crested with glory's cry. No,
I take that back. You gushed, refused
to follow directions. And still refuse.
They call it spirited. Thin boned,
your waking cough rattles my sleep.
How does one so slight, so misfired,
charge through every stop?
Even now you leave me
bit by bit
a baby tooth cocooned in tissue
a lock a note
why should I submit
to this sentiment?
because you come to me
mouth wide
bragging
about what is so close
to gone

Hiding the Symptoms

Gulls flock the Food Lion
parking lot. My son
asks what animal
I would choose
to come back as.
I answer *bird.*
Then I'm winging what's left
of my bone weary self
over the evergreens,
afraid to look
down or up.

In the Schenectady of the Mind

I hung with boys
who had no brothers.
We pedaled our Schwinns
to the reservoir
or downtown
to the forbidden zone
where Last Tango in Paris
was showing
at the old vaudeville house.
We eyed locked cases
in shops without signs,
dreaming of knives.

In the Schenectady
of the mind, I trudge
slushy sidewalks,
waiting for ghost boys
to zip by, propelled
by red metal wings.

Hand Basket

The kitchen table is cluttered
with red paper, glue, tissue,
glitter. My daughter tells me
about her boyfriend, how she loves him
but sometimes he bothers her
too much. I remember crushes
that made my teeth chatter,
where my senses were mussed
by miss charm-of-the-hour.
It didn't matter that she
couldn't hear the strafe and rattle
that tore me apart. Just as it
doesn't matter to my daughter
that the world is going to hell
in a hand basket, as long
as it's full of cut paper hearts.

Grand Mal

Raining again, puddles pock
the saturated yard.
I search for tools—hammer, nails,
a saw—to begin the ark.
The dog follows my every move.
She wants to be sure
she is one of the selected. Once,
my brother and I dammed
a schoolyard creek—sticks, rocks,
mud. Serious as sin,
we shouted at every break
and scurried to patch weak spots.
We worked beyond the reach
of Mother's call. Last night,
the dog had a seizure.
In the family room dark,
I held her where she had fallen,
unable to stand, eyes rolled back,
a puddle on the hardwood floor.
I held her like a lover,
a child, a brother gone
ten years, until the shaking
stopped and she grew still
as sleep. The only sound
the ragged breath of rain.

Put Down

I believe in the power
of coincidence. The night
my first son was born,
our Samoyed had six pups.
At 4 am in pouring rain,
I found them in a muddy hole.

It might be easy to tell
how the dog looks at me,
years later, as I drive her
to the vet. After all,
she is just a dog. But there
is something about the way
her ears go flat when she thinks
I disapprove of her
instead of death, how she knows
just when to push into my hand.

Whosoever

The pain in my knuckles is a greeting
from beyond, a cloud freckled sky.
Even weather hides behind the not so tall
buildings that tell a story, a life.
Nuns peddle down main, white shoes flash

the gravel god voice of wheel and spoke.
The pain in my shoulders is my father
so long gone his whiskers have forgotten
the perfume of barley and rye. He rides
and whispers into my hair—everything,

whosoever. The pain in my knees
is nothing but love, a thimble, a thread I tug
each day from your favorite blue sweater
that will eventually disappear and I,
finding the only door unlocked, will follow.

Thinking about My Father's Hands before
    a Storm

This morning I watched a little bird chase
a much bigger bird across the sky.

I should be able to tell what kinds of birds
they were, knowing how you desire specifics.

But they were too far away, black winged
shadows against white, the sky

that is making room for a storm now.
Birds are hiding. I am hiding too. I know

soon the dog will huddle beneath my every step,
and finally the windows will rattle and the rain

will come to wash away whatever there is
that needs cleansing. For some reason, I'm thinking

about my father's hands. How he wrapped them tightly
around his drink when he came home from work,

home from the world I knew so little about.
After the second drink, his face would loosen.

It was as if storm clouds were leaving his face.
I think about his hands, how wrinkled they seemed,

how he would put them on my shoulders when he thought
I needed comfort. I still can feel them sometimes.

And if I looked out the window now, I'm sure
I would see them flapping across the sky

like unnamed birds chasing away this dark weather.

The Window

We dust what shows—candles without flame, figurines
frozen in dance. Rituals exhausted, we wait

for our guests. It doesn't take much to slip back
to second grade where Mrs. Goldfarb clears her throat

eternally, where the faceless boy wets his pants, pissing
a stream that threatens to carry us away. Or further

back to where the yard is a jungle, where we claw
mossy earth or risk being sucked into darkness

that waits like a deaf grandmother. If we looked
into windows bleeding light, we'd see ourselves passing

photographs. Looking out we'd see trees flamed
purple against a moon-dashed sky. One of us

might notice rustling in the underbrush, by the birdbath
an untied shoe, a pile of discarded clothes, an embrace

of shirt sleeves, before they turn back into leaves
and we turn back to refill an empty glass.

The Night Stevie Wonder Saved My Life

horns erupt
my daughter marionettes
to the backbeat
bounds around
the room
then I am swinging her
so fast knickknacks totter
figurines shimmy shake
out of nowhere
my wife appears
twisting as wildly
as the rug allows
dancing out of breath
laughing because for at least
two minutes and fifty seconds
this is it
the whole house jumping
the singer so sure
everything is alright
and maybe just maybe he's right

About the Author

Jim Zola is a poet and photographer living in North Carolina.

www.ingramcontent.com/pod-product-compliance
Lightning Source LLC
Chambersburg PA
CBHW022013080426
42733CB00007B/583